Regal Musical Instruments Volume Two:
Addendum and Errata

By Bob Carlin

Book Design by Steve Terrill

ISBN: 978-1-57424-412-0

P.O. Box 17878 - Anaheim Hills, CA 92817
www.centerstream-usa.com • (714) 779-9390

Photograph by Matthew Spencer

Thanks! and Sources: Take Two

Thanks to eBay, Fred Oster and Catherine Jacobs/Vintage Instruments, Eric Schoenberg/Schoenberg Guitars, Wil Bremer and the late Julie Luther/Spruce Tree Music, realguitars.com, Leo Coulson/Intermountain Guitar, George Saich, Kerry Char/Char Lutheries, Neil Reck, the late Scott Freilich/Top Shelf Music, Steve Kovacik/Kovacik Guitars, Gayle Dean Wardlow, Stan Werbin and Dave Machette/Elderly Instruments, Mark Demaray, Andrew Nair, J. T. Fisher, Dave Portman, John Bernunzio/Bernunzio Uptown Music, Steve Uhrik and Peter Kohman/Retrofret, Philip Reed, Worshaw Collection/Smithsonian Institution, Walter and Christy Carter/Carter Vintage Guitars, Jake Wildwood/Antebellum Instruments, and Gary N. Schultz.

The Regal Manufacturing Company, Indianapolis, IN, 1901. Music Trade Review, *April 6, 1901, courtesy of NARAS.*

Regal Made Instruments: A 2021 Update

I authored the first book-length study of Regal Musical Instruments knowing it would be a preliminary attempt at making sense out of the convoluted history and products of that company. As expected, I had to be content with "hitting the highlights." Since that time, the book has served as a catalyst for drawing instruments and information "out of the woodwork." While the current Addendum and Errata still only covers a fraction of Regal's output, I believe this additional data helps to more fully draw a picture of the Regal story.

As with before, I take full responsibility for the material presented herein. You the reader are always welcome to contact me with corrections and additions through the publisher.

—Bob Carlin, Lexington, NC, September 1, 2021.

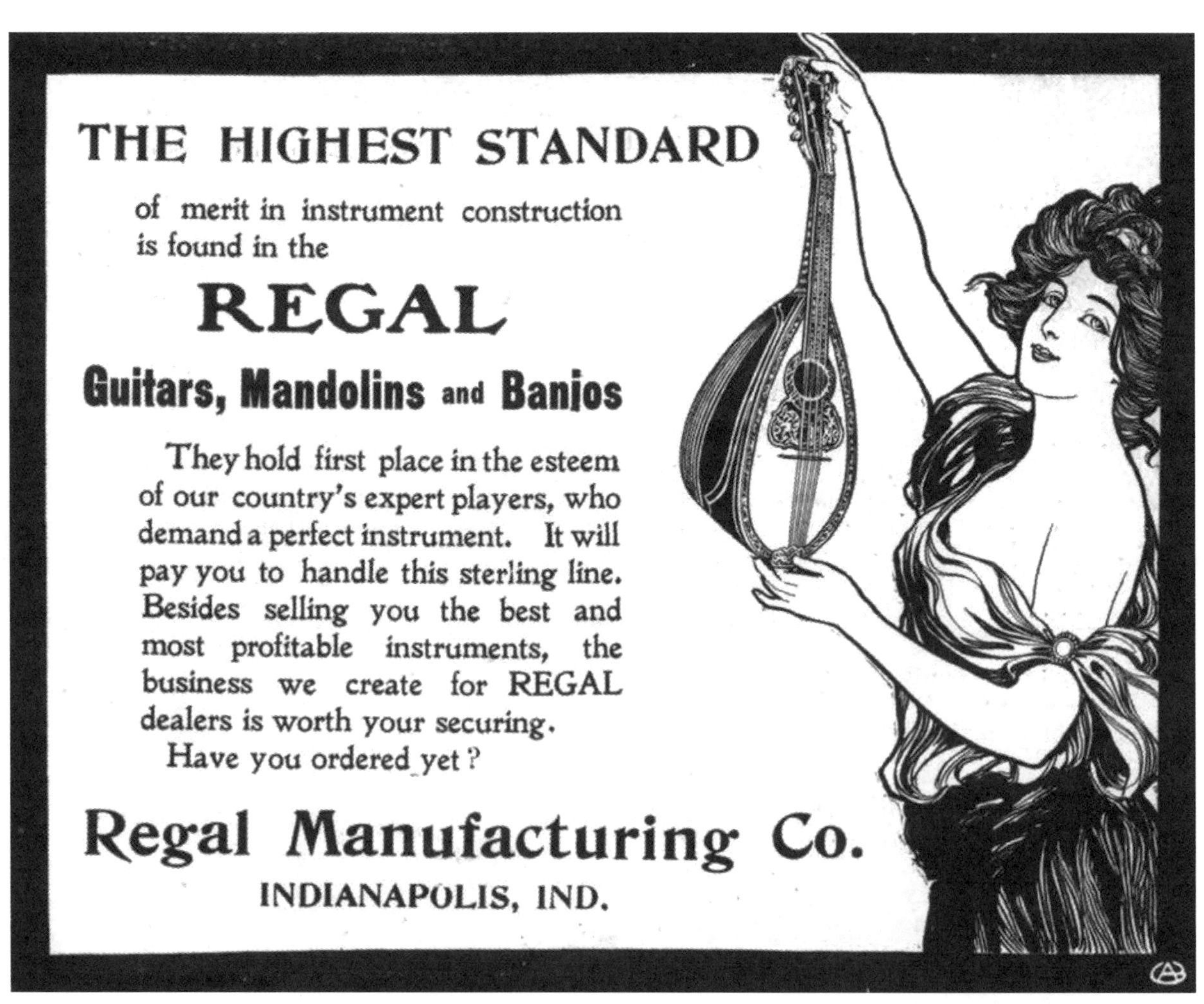

Advertisement, "The Highest Standard," Music Trade Review, *January 25, 1902. Courtesy NARAS.*

Table of Contents

Chapter One: The Birth of Regal Redux

"Ye Troubadour Would Have Fared Much Better In His Love Affairs Had He Possessed a Regal Mandolin or Guitar."

—From trade card, Wulschner & Son, N.D.

In 1901, Regal was sold by the Wulschner family to a group of Indianapolis businessmen. When the decision was made to introduce other "cheaper" grade instruments, the new Regal company ran the following advertisement:

> *Regal musical instruments have the deserved reputation of being the finest in the world, both as for workmanship and tone. They are, however, a little higher in price than others, and many mandolin and guitar players desire a less expensive instrument, at the same time preferring The Regal make and guarantee of quality. We are, therefore, going to place a cheaper line of mandolins and guitars on the market. To the person sending us the best name for this second line of instruments before November 30th, 1901, we will make a present of either Style No. 23 Regal Mandolin, or Style No. 115 Regal Guitar. Each instrument retails everywhere for $125.00 and cannot be had for less.*
>
> *Failing to win the prize, each person who sends us a name will receive, free, our booklets, 'A Regal Rhapsody' and "Regal Friends,' containing portraits of the celebrated players as well as copies of the Regal Mandolin March, the Regal Banjo March and the Regal Gavotte for guitar solo.—Ad, Regal Manufacturing Company, No. 24 S. Capitol Avenue, Indianapolis, IND.*

The Three White Kuhns (sic) with guitar shaped mandolin, harp guitar and large bodied guitar. Hand dated November 6, 1911, Hippodrome, Cleveland, Ohio. Photograph by Apeda Studio, New York, NY. Robert, Charles and Paul Kuhn performed in vaudeville from around 1907 through at least the early 1930s. The instruments in this photograph were probably made sometime prior to the image. Collection of the author.

Chapter Two: **Regal in Chicago**

LYON & HEALY, CHICAGO.

No. ____________ ORIGINAL.–Please sign and return this to LYON & HEALY.

In Effect August 1st, 1905.
(All Previous Contracts Cancelled.)

Selling Contract

In Consideration *of receiving reduced prices on* **Regal Guitars and Mandolins** ____________ *hereby agree with LYON & HEALY not to sell any style of said Instruments at a less price than indicated for the proper number in the following Price List:*

GUITARS	
100 S—Standard	$15 00
101 S—Standard	20 00
101 C—Concert Grand	22 50
101 A—Auditorium	25 00
109 S—Standard	35 00
109 C—Concert Grand	40 00
111 S—Standard	45 00
111 C—Concert Grand	50 00

MANDOLINS	
0	$15 00
1	20 00
7	25 00
15	35 00
19	50 00

Except to Professional Teachers of these instruments, and that to them ____________ will not allow a greater discount than 20 per cent.

It is understood that the above is the only exception, and does not refer to dealers, the manufacturers desiring to supply them direct, that they may control the prices and protect the trade, therefore ____________ agree not to supply any other dealer or dealers at less than retail prices under any circumstances ____________ also agree not to present, or otherwise include gratis, articles of value in the price of these instruments, such as cases, instruction books, with the exception of "Free Lessons," as provided in the next paragraph, etc.

Permission to Include Free Lessons *is given to dealers at their option, at their own expense, to give "free lessons" with a Regal, provided no commission is paid to a teacher on such instrument, and that the cost of the said lessons to the dealer does not exceed 20 per cent. of the selling price. In other words—"free lessons" may be substituted for a teacher's commission. No other extras of any nature whatsoever may be given or included with Regals.*

Note—A plan, "How to arrange with local teachers to give 'free lessons,'" and a series of strong newspaper advertisements will be furnished gratis to all dealers by our Publicity Department. In connection with "free lessons," please observe that through this means, we have increased our own retail business in mandolins, guitars and banjos fourfold. Any live dealer can do the same.

____________ also agree to change said retail prices, in case it becomes necessary from time to time, to conform to the Manufacturer's retail list, it being understood that a thirty days' notice of such changes shall be given, and that all changes shall be uniform to all dealers throughout the country. It is understood as a consideration in this contract that LYON & HEALY will strictly adhere to the above prices in their sales to private and professional customers.

Dated this ____________ day of ____________ 190____

at ____________

Lyon & Healy

Signed ____________

Page from 1906 Lyon & Healy catalogue, with information about the newly acquired Regal instruments. Collection of the author.

Regal Musical Instrument Co., work force outside of the Chicago factory, November 5, 1934. Notice there are only forty-five workers including management. Joe Phetteplace is fifth from the left sitting in the front row. My guess is that the two men in suits standing sixth and eighth from the left in the back row are Herman Schlitt and Frank Kordick. Courtesy Larry Phetteplace.

We now know, thanks to descendant Gary Schultz, the names for a few more of the workers shown in the company photograph. Schultz's ancestors include John Athanasius Schultz (1884-1967, extreme left, sitting in the first row), and John's youngest child, Frank Louis Schultz (1914-1995, standing in the back row, seventh from the right). To Frank Louis's right is possibly his in-law, John E. Swanson, Sr. According to Gary, the Schultz's were a musical family, and he provided pictures of Frank's brother George (1911-1987) with various Regal-made guitars. After previous careers as a piano finisher and vaudevillian, John A. Schultz joined Regal in 1923.

Gary also graciously provided photographs, made in 2021, of the loading dock where the employee portrait was made as it looks today, as well as a modern-day view of the catalogue image reprinted on p25 of my original book on Regal. Collection/photographs by Gary Schultz.

Regal Musical Instrument Co., Chicago factory, from the 1934 catalogue, courtesy Ron Middlebrook.

Chapter Three: Mandolins

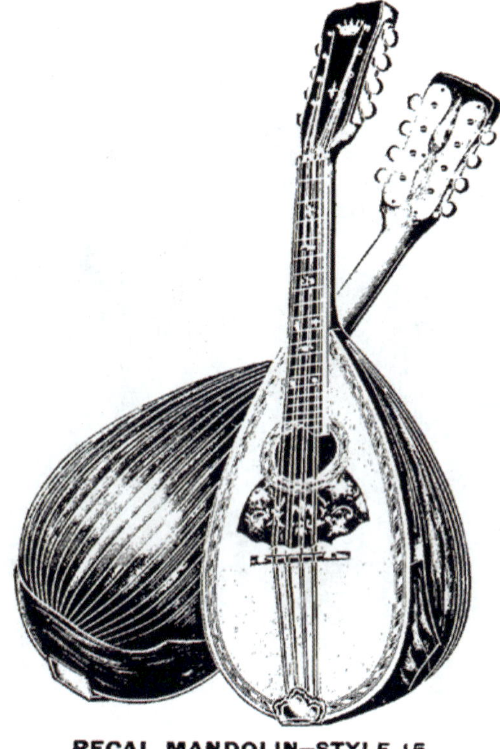

REGAL MANDOLIN—STYLE 15.

Rosewood, twenty-four ribs, white holly strips between each rib; mahogany neck; oval ebony fingerboard bound with celluloid and beautifully inlaid with pearl ornaments; ebony veneered head-piece ornamented with pearl; sound-hole and edges bound with celluloid and inlaid; guardplate ornamented with a beautiful pearl design; tail-piece handsomely engraved; nickel plated plateheads, handsomely engraved.

Highly French polished, each..........$43 75

Photographs of bowl back mandolin by the author.

REGAL MANDOLINS.

REGAL MANDOLIN, STYLE O.

Rosewood, eleven ribs, colored wood strips inlaid between each rib; mahogany neck; oval ebony finger-board, with pearl ornaments in the positions; ebony veneered head-piece, ornamented with a pearl crown; sound-hole bound with celluloid and inlaid; celluloid binding and inlaying around top edge, nickel plated and engraved patent heads.

Highly French polished, each..............$18 75

Style O.

One Hundred Lesson Certificate Free with all Regal Mandolins.

REGAL MANDOLIN, STYLE I.

Rosewood, thirteen ribs, colored wood strips between each rib; mahogany neck; oval ebony finger-board, with pearl ornaments in the positions; ebony veneered head-piece; sound-hole bound with celluloid and inlaid; celluloid binding around top edge; nickel plated covered patent heads; nickel plated tail-piece.

Highly French polished, each.............$25 00

REGAL MANDOLIN, STYLE 7.

Rosewood, fifteen ribs, white holly strips between each rib; mahogany neck; oval ebony finger-board bound with celluloid and inlaid with pearl ornaments in the positions; ebony veneered head-piece ornamented with pearl; sound-hole and edges bound with celluloid and inlaid; nickel plated tail-piece; covered plate-heads.

Highly French polished, each.............$31 25

Style 1.

Style 7.

For Retail Selling Prices See Copy of Contract on Back Page.

From 1906 Lyon & Healy catalogue. Collection of the author.

Around the time that Lyon & Healy spun off Regal, a new, more ornate label was introduced. This large paper mandolin sound hole oval contained red printing, with "Chicago" and a one-year guarantee. Photograph by Matthew Spencer. Collection of the author.

Flat Back Mandolins

Instrument: Mandolin.

Model(s): Kordick patent design reverse scroll.

Years Made: 1914-1935.

Brand: Stella.

Quality: Low grade.

Logos Used: (Unusual) Stella paper headstock label, "Lyra" in black on white plastic plate top of headstock horizontally, Victoria/B&J paper soundhole label.

Patent drawing, "F. Kordick, Musical Instrument. Application Filed July 10, 1914."

"Flat-Back:/Mandolin No. 101," Progressive Musical Instrument Corporation (PMD) catalogue, circa 1928. Courtesy the National Music Museum

PMI No. 101

Instrument: Mandolin.

Model(s): PMI No. 101.

Years Made: 1915-1937.

Brand(s): Clifford and Vernon.

Quality: Low grade.

Measurements: 9 ½" across the body and 2 ½-3" deep.

Logos Used: "The Vernon" on celluloid headstock plate.

Schultz No. 2216

Instrument: Mandolin.

Model: Schultz No. 2216.

Brand(s): Kingston.

Quality: Low.

Logos Used: "Kingston" white stencil vertically on headstock.

Perfacktone No. 2917

Instrument: Mandolin.

Model(s): Perfacktone No. 2917.

Brand(s): S. S. Stewart.

Quality: Low to mid-grade.

Measurements: Overall length is 24", body is 9 ⅛" wide, 2 ⅝" deep with a 13 ¼" scale.

Logos Used: "S. S. Stewart" in script on tuner coverplate, blue S. S. Stewart paper soundhole label, green Regal headstock decal.

Some came with the same pickguard as model 2923. Later Regal-labeled models utilized the "rabbit ears/tulip" headstock shape.

2917—**Perfacktone** Mandolin, **genuine mahogany** body with finest mahogany top to match. Large inlaid guard plate at soundhole, genuine mahogany neck, ebony extension fingerboard. Top and bottom edges inlaid with neat black and white purfling. Patent heads are **protected with nickel plated shield**.......Each **$19.00**

" Perfacktone Lute Mandolins," "No, 2917" made by Regal. Progressive Musical Instrument Corporation (PMI) catalogue, circa 1928. Courtesy the National Music Museum.

Schultz No. 2213

Instrument: Mandolin.

Model(s): Regal "Superior," Schultz No. 2213, 2361 and PMI No. 114.

Brand(s): Victoria, Bruno.

Quality: Good.

Measurements: Total body length 24", 9" across the body, 13" scale and 1 ⅛" nut width.

Logos Used: B&J Victoria paper soundhole label, "C. Bruno New York" stamped in headstock back, C. Bruno and Son black paper soundhole label, "Bruno" inlaid in headstock, engraved "Washburn" in script on tuner coverplate, S. S. Stewart blue paper soundhole label, "S. S. Stewart, Maker" stamped in headstock back.

"Regal Flat-Back Mandolins" "No. 2213," H. C. Schultz catalogue, 1928. Courtesy Stan Werbin/Elderly Instruments.

"REGAL" Flat-Back Mandolin No. 110 as pictured above. Genuine rosewood back and sides; spruce top with large tortoise celluloid guard plate inlaid at side of sound hole; guard plate inlaid with white celluloid floral design; genuine mahogany neck with rosewood veneered head; fine extension finger board bound with celluloid; handsomely inlaid around sound hole and edges with neat black and white veneer lines; compensating bridge; best trimmings; hand rubbed and polished.

Style Number 110 *Price $24.00*

PMI No. 110

Instrument: Mandolin.

Model: PMI No. 110, Harwood "Artist," Ditson "Victory."

Brand(s): Wurlitzer, Bruno.

Quality: High.

Logos Used: "S. S. Stewart" on headstock in pearl, S. S. Stewart blue paper soundhole label, Wurlitzer paper soundhole label, Bruno paper soundhole label.

◄*"Flat-Back Mandolin No. 110," Progressive Musical Instrument Corporation (PMI) catalogue, circa 1928. Courtesy the National Music Museum.*

Perfacktone 2923

Instrument: Mandolin.

Model: Perfacktone 2923.

Special Features: "Batwing" pickguard and "heart" peghead shape.

The Perfacktone 2923 appears to be a version of PMI No. 110. Schultz No. 2223 uses the same pickguard and peghead shape. Another variant with what appears to be faux rosewood back and sides was sold under the "Rex" (Gretsch) brand.

" Perfacktone Lute Mandolins," "No, 2293" made by Regal. Progressive Musical Instrument Corporation (PMI) catalogue, circa 1928. Courtesy the National Music Museum.

Schultz No. 2223

Instrument: Mandolin.

Model: Regal "Superior," Schultz No. 2223, Harwood "Artist."

Brand(s): Rex, Bruno, S. S. Stewart.

Logos Used: Rex paper soundhole label, "Bruno Mandolin" paper soundhole label, S. S. Stewart blue paper soundhole label, "S. S. Stewart" engraved script on tuner cover.

"Regal Flat-Back Mandolins" "No. 2223," H. C. Schultz catalogue, 1928. Courtesy Stan Werbin/Elderly Instruments..

Custom Built

Instrument: Mandolin.

Model(s): Kingston.

Measurements: 9 ¾" wide and 3" deep.

Logos Used: "Kingston" vertically on headstock in white stencil.

"Regal Flat-Back Mandolins" "No. 2224," H. C. Schultz catalogue, 1928. Courtesy Stan Werbin/Elderly Instruments.

Two Point

Instrument: Mandolin.

Model: "Venetian" Flat Back Two Point.

Brand(s): Regal, San Jose.

Quality: Low.

Special Features: Some with "tulip" headstock shape, floating pickguard and sunburst back, sides and neck.

Woods: Some with poplar neck.

Measurements: 24" total length, 10" width and 2 ¼" deep.

Logos Used: Green Regal headstock decal, "San Jose, B. H. & S. N.Y." paper soundhole label.

Schultz 2224

Instrument: Mandolin.

Brand(s): Stahl, American Conservatory.

Measurements: 9 ¾" wide, 2" deep, with a 13" scale and a 1 ⅛" wide nut.

Logos Used: "Wm. C. Stahl, Milwaukee, WI" paper soundhole label, American Conservatory paper soundhole label, Regal headstock medallion in pearl on later versions.

Two models of Regal-made Bacon mandolins, a "B&D Ramona" and a "B&D Sultana Grand," shown in the 1937 Chicago Musical instrument (CMI) catalogue. Courtesy the National Music Museum.

Modified Kordick Shape

Instrument: Mandolin.

Model: Modified Kordick patent shape.

Years Made: 1936-1939.

Brand(s): Regal, B&D, Maurer.

Quality: Low to high grade.

Special Features: Arched top, carved on higher grade instruments, "F" holes on some models.

Woods: Spruce over maple, mahogany neck (B&D).

Measurements: 13 ¾" scale, 1 3/16" nut width, 10 ⅜" wide, 3 ¼" deep.

Logos Used: Oval paper soundhole label, various Bacon model designations on headstock, Maurer stamp inside, green headstock decal (1939).

Known Original List Price: $12.00-135.00 wholesale, $8.45-13.50 retail.

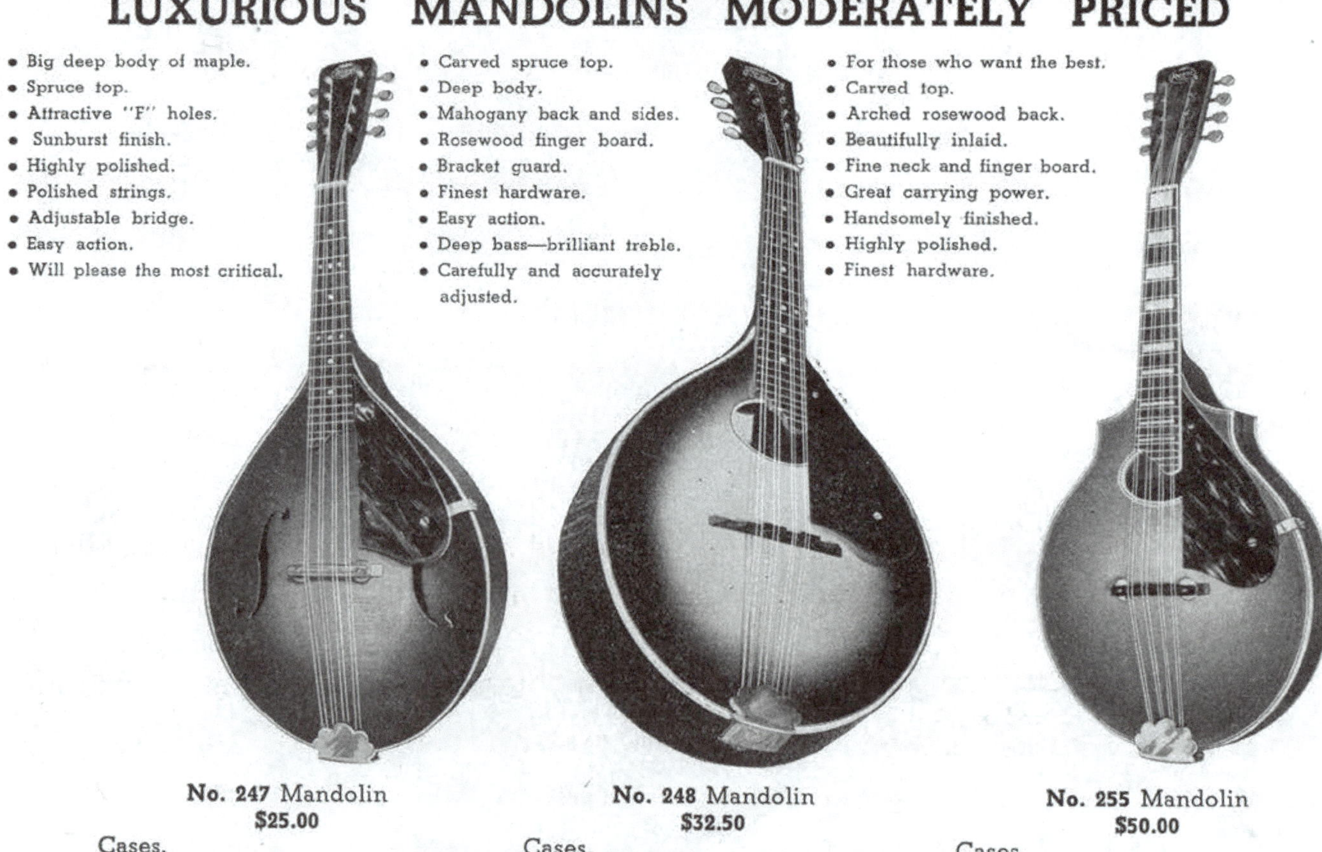

From the 1939 Regal catalogue, collection of the author.

Arched Top

Measurements: 13 ¾" scale, 1 3/16" nut width, 10 ⅜" wide, 3 ¼" deep.

Logos Used: Oval paper soundhole label, various Bacon model designations on headstock, Maurer stamp inside, green headstock decal (1939).

Known Original List Price: $12.00-135.00 wholesale, $8.45-13.50 retail.

Guitar Bodied Mandolin

Instrument: Mandolin.

Model: Guitar-mandola, mandolina, guitar-mandolin, "Serenata," "Royal."

Years Made: 1901-1932.

Brand(s): 20th Century, Regal, Royal.

Quality: Low grade.

Special Features: Scaled down guitar body shape, painted body some models.

Woods: Quartered sawn oak back and sides on some versions.

Measurements: The overall length is 21 ½-22", lower bout 8-8 ¼" wide, upper bout 5 ½-5 ¾" wide, scale length 13 ⅛", nut width 1 ⅛", and body depth at the neck joint is 2 ½" (Royal).

Logos Used: Royal decal on headstock, circular Regal decal on headstock.

THE 20TH CENTURY GUITAR-MANDOLIN

STYLE 212

Maple, Dark Cherry Finish, mahogany finished neck, ebonized finger-board and bridge, pearl posi- celluloid guard plate, sound hole fancily inlaid and bevelled, top edge fancily inlaid and bound with oid, a fancily inlaid stripe down back, American patent heads, finely hand polished.

Price, $8.13.

Regal Manufacturing Co, Indianapolis, catalogue, 1907, The 20th Century Guitar-Mandolin Style 212. Photographs by Jim Bollman, courtesy Stu Cohen.

Chapter Four: **Harp Guitars and 12 Strings**

Double Neck Hawaiian Guitar

Instrument: Double neck Hawaiian guitar.

Years Made: 1917/conversion circa 1935.

Quality: High.

Special features: Harp guitar converted at the factory to a double-neck (both necks fretted) Hawaiian guitar.

Woods: Natural spruce top, rosewood back and sides, mahogany necks.

Measurements: Upper bout 12", waist 10 1/4", lower bout 16 3/8", depth at end block 4 1/2", depth at upper block 3 7/8", scale length 25 2/8".

Logos Used: None.

This harp guitar converted to a "Hawaiian" double neck guitar has got to be one of the stranger instruments to come out of the Regal shop. It is very similar to Lyon & Healy's Lakeside Jumbo and American Conservatory Style 2210 harp guitar catalogued in 1917 and shown in Hubert Pleijsier's book on Washburn (p50). The guitar sports neither a Regal label nor one from L&H. HOWEVER, due to the shared Red Dragon decalcomania found on Regal ukes from 1935 (p279-280), Wil Bremer of Spruce Tree Music believes this hybrid Hawaiian to be a Regal product. The top and soundhole are bound in white with colored marquetry, and the soundhole also sports a fine line rosette. The back as well is bound with a center stripe. The heelcap is rosewood and the tuners for both necks are three-on-a-plate square enders with top mounted gears.

Photographs, courtesy Spruce Tree Music, shows the guitar and ukulele featuring Red Dragon decalcomania.

"No. R 90 Harp Guitar" and "No. 615-12," Tonk Bros. catalogue,1937, courtesy Tony Marcus; Regal Musical Instrument catalogue, 1937, courtesy The National Music Museum.

Model R 90

Instrument: Harp guitar or contra bass guitar.

Model: No. Regal 90 harp guitar.

Years Made: 1935-1937.

Brand(s): Regal.

Quality: High.

Special features: A regular guitar neck of six strings plus a "contra-bass" neck of six strings. Construction similar to model No. 1932 carved top regular guitar shown on p231.

Woods: Spruce over mahogany, mahogany neck.

Logos Used: "Regal" in pearl script in bottom neck and green Regal headstock decal in top neck.

Known Original Wholesale Price: $90.00.

12 String Guitars

I was unable to write anything about Regal-made 12 string guitars in the first edition of Regal Musical Instruments due to a lack of definitive information. The situation on 12 strings hasn't improved much. What follows is my first, albeit incomplete, stab at making sense out of Regal manufactured 12 string guitars.

Two coursed guitars built between the late 1920s and mid-1930s have turned up on the internet that were definitely by Regal. Unfortunately, lacking high resolution images of either, a description will have to suffice for this volume.

The first was a part of Regal's "custom built" line, and includes the custom built paper soundhole label. The guitar features a spruce top bound in black with fine lines around the top and soundhole, mahogany sides and back with black binding and back stripe. Dimensions are: lower bout 15 ¼", upper bout 11 ¼", a 24 ¾" scale, 4" deep at the endpin and a nut width of 1 ⅞".

The second example, while unlabeled, exhibits details found on other Regal six string guitars of the period. This guitar has a natural spruce top bound in white with fine lines around the top and soundhole and a floating pickguard made of composite material. The bridge is also floating with a tailpiece partially covering a decorative decal. The sides and back are birch, with a large decalcomania covering the back. The headstock is slotted. The lower bout measures 14 11/16", upper bout 10 7/16", body length is 19 ⅞, depth at neck 3 ⅜", depth at end block 3 ⅞" with a scale length of 26".

12 String Version Of Oahu Faux Painted

Instrument: 12 String Version of Oahu Faux Painted Guitar.

Model: 12 string.

Years Made: 1930-1934.

Quality: Medium.

Special features: Decalcomania vines and flowers.

Woods: Natural spruce over birch, poplar neck.

Logos Used: None.

With decalcomania like the guitar discussed on p187 of my original Regal book, this slot-headed, 12 fret guitar features 18 total frets, an (unoriginal) floating bridge and tailpiece setup, natural spruce top bound in white and a white bound soundhole with marquetry.

Regal Model 615-12

Instrument: 12-string guitar.

Model: Regal 615-12.

Years Made: 1937-1939.

Brand(s): Regal.

Quality: Medium.

Special features: Ladder braced, decalcomania backstripe, top and soundhole bound in white and marquetry.

Woods: Natural spruce top, birch back and sides.

Measurements: Lower bout 16 ¼", upper bout 11 ¾", 4 3/8" deep at end block, overall length of body is 20 5/8", 25 ¼" scale, 2" nut ("Jumbo" size).

Logos Used: Paper Regal soundhole label, headstock decal of some sort.

Regal

Regal Model 612

Instrument: 12-string guitar.

Model: Regal 612.

Years Made: 1949/50.

Brand(s): Regal.

Quality: Medium.

Special features: Solid headstock, white bound ladder braced top and back, white heel cap, floating bridge, six on plate tuners, trapeze tailpiece, 3 piece neck, 12 frets to the body, 19 frets total.

Woods: Natural spruce top, mahogany back and sides, rosewood fingerboard.

Measurements: 15 ⅛-½" lower bout, 25 ½"' scale, 4" deep, 2" wide nut and 19 ¼" long body ("Auditorium" size).

Logos Used: Multi-colored headstock decal, "Regal" white headstock stencil.

Known Original Price: $36.00.

◄Headstock, and full frontal view. Courtesy Real Guitars, San Francisco, CA.

►Victor N. Cabas, Jr. (1949-2018) was a fixture at guitar shows throughout the United States. Although he never met a vintage guitar that he didn't like, Cabas was particularly drawn to the "catalog guitars" from the first half of the 20th century. Victor felt that these "guitars of the people" suited the acoustic blues that he performed. At the time of his death, his "collection" numbered over one thousand instruments. His larger-then-life personality has yet to be filled by any up-and-coming dealer/collectors. Photograph by the author.

Chapter Five: Banjos

Since the release of *Regal Musical Instruments*, four banjos labeled "Regal/Indianapolis" have surfaced. The only difference between three of them is the amount of headstock inlay. Otherwise, they are identical. All utilize brackets that attach around the bottom of the ebonized rim featuring an outside band of marquetry and white binding inside, black heelcap and a twenty-two fret ebonized fingerboard with star inlays at frets 3, 5, 7, 10, 12, 14 and 17.

Regal Mfg. Co., Indianapolis

Instrument: Five-String Banjo.

Model: Five-String Banjo.

Years Made: 1901-1904.

Brand(s): Regal.

Quality: Good.

Special Features: Twenty-two shoeless brackets.

Woods: Ebony fingerboard, cherry neck, laminate pot.

Measurements: 11 ⅝" rim diameter, 27" scale, 1 ¼" width of fingerboard at nut.

(pages 26-29) Photographs, an amalgam of images from two of the instruments cited, show the Regal dowel stick label and back of the rim, as well as headstock detail and head tightening rim hardware. Banjos courtesy Joe Hornung and Art Meisel, photographs by the author.

REGAL

Chapter Six: **Flattop Guitars**

(pages 30-32) This extremely ornate ladder-braced instrument features a 14" lower bout, is labeled as a Wulschner/Regal and stamped inside with the number "671-15." Views include full-front and back, headstock front and back, with close-ups of the bridge and tuners. Guitar courtesy Paula Hurst of Logan, Utah (the guitar belonged to her grandfather), with photographs courtesy Leo Coulson/Intermountain Guitar & Banjo, Salt Lake City, UT.

(pages 33-35) This guitar is equivalent to a Montgomery Ward "Artists'" model. I've also seen other high-end Regal-made guitars from this time period sporting the SS Stewart gold headstock decal and Stewart blue oval or "Thorough-Bred" paper soundhole label. However, I'm still not 100% convinced that this instrument came out of the Regal facility. Photographs show full front and back views, along with close-ups of the top binding and headstock. Courtesy Kerry Char/Char Lutheries, Portland, OR.

GUITARS.

One Hundred Lesson Certificate Free with all Regal Guitars.

REGAL GUITAR—STYLE 109.

Rosewood, mahogany neck, oval ebony finger-board, bound with celluloid and very handsomely inlaid with pearl designs; head-piece veneered with ebony, pearl crown inlaid, bound with celluloid and inlaid with pearl ornaments; sound-hole and edges, both front and back, bound with celluloid; top edge and sound-hole handsomely inlaid with fancy colored woods, a very handsome inlaid stripe down back and under endpin; ebony bridge, nickel plated patent heads engraved. Highly French polished.

Style 109S—Standard Size..............$37 50

One Hundred Lesson Certificate Free with all Regal Guitars.

REGAL GUITAR—STYLE 111.

Rosewood, mahogany neck, oval ebony finger-board, bound with celluloid and elaborately inlaid with rich pearl designs; head-piece veneered with ebony and bound with celluloid, both front and back, and inlaid with pearl crown; sound-hole and edges, both front and back, bound with celluloid and elaborately inlaid with beautiful colored woods; two strips of celluloid inlaid down back and under endpin; ebony bridge, nickel plated patent heads, celluloid buttons. Highly French polished.

Style 111S—Standard Size........... $56 25

For Retail Selling Prices See Copy of Contract on Back Page.

Two pages from a 1906 Lyon & Healy catalogue showing Regal guitars. Collection of the author.

GUITARS.

REGAL GUITAR—STYLE 100.

Rosewood, mahogany neck, oval ebony finger-board, pearl positions; ebony veneered head-piece; pearl crown inlaid, sound-hole celluloid bound and inlaid; top edge inlaid and bound with rosewood, inlaid stripe down back and under endpin; ebony bridge; nickel plated and engraved patent heads. Highly French polished.

Style 100—Standard Size......$18 75

One Hundred Lesson Certificate Free with all Regal Guitars.

REGAL GUITAR—STYLE 101

Rosewood, mahogany neck, oval ebony finger-board, pearl position dots; ebony veneered headpiece, pearl crown inlaid; sound-hole and top edge inlaid and bound with celluloid; beautiful inlaid stripe down back and under endpin; ebony bridge; nickel plated patent heads engraved. Highly French polished.

Style 101S—Standard Size.........$25 00
Style 101A—Auditorium Size...... 31 25

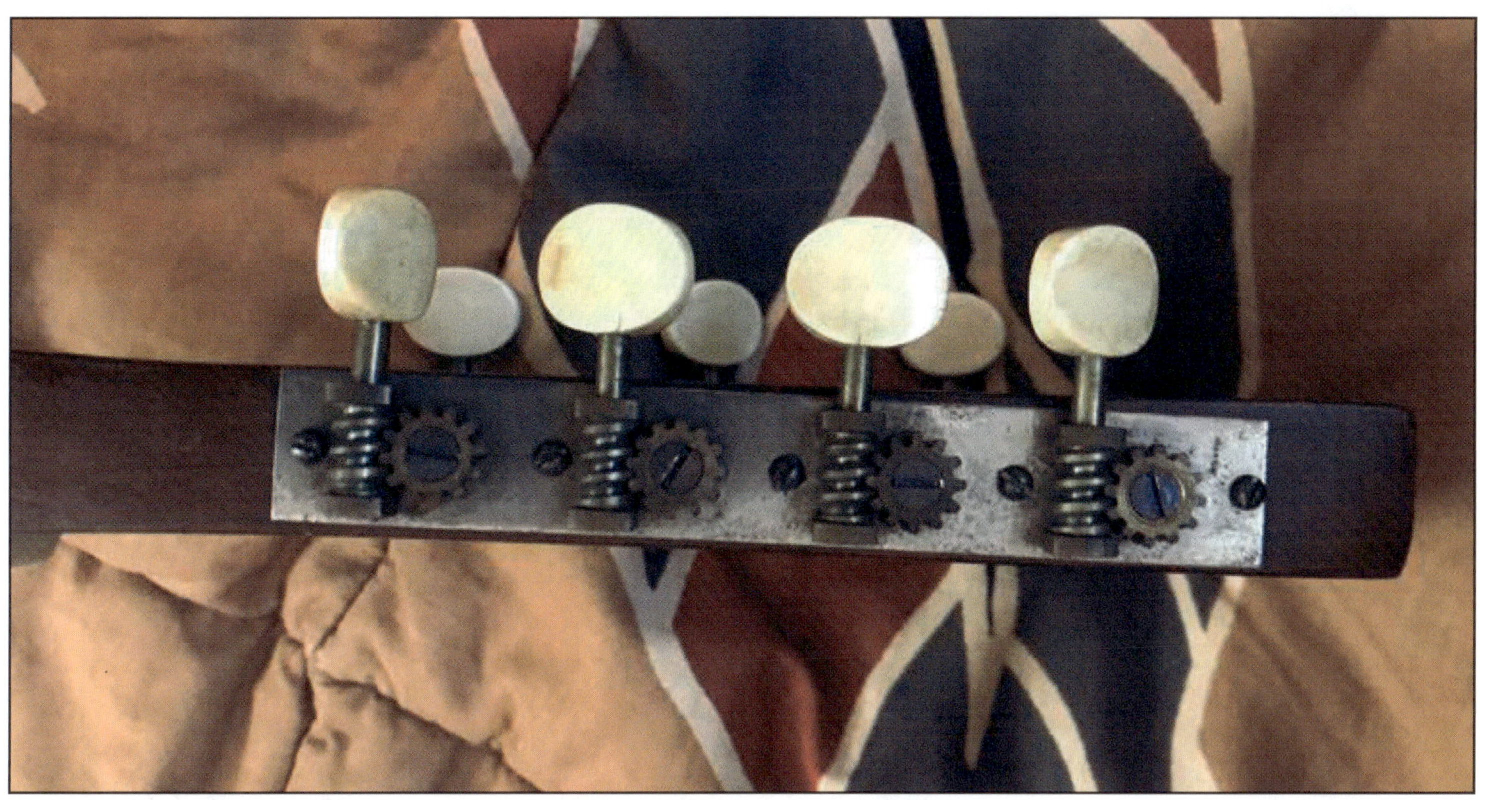

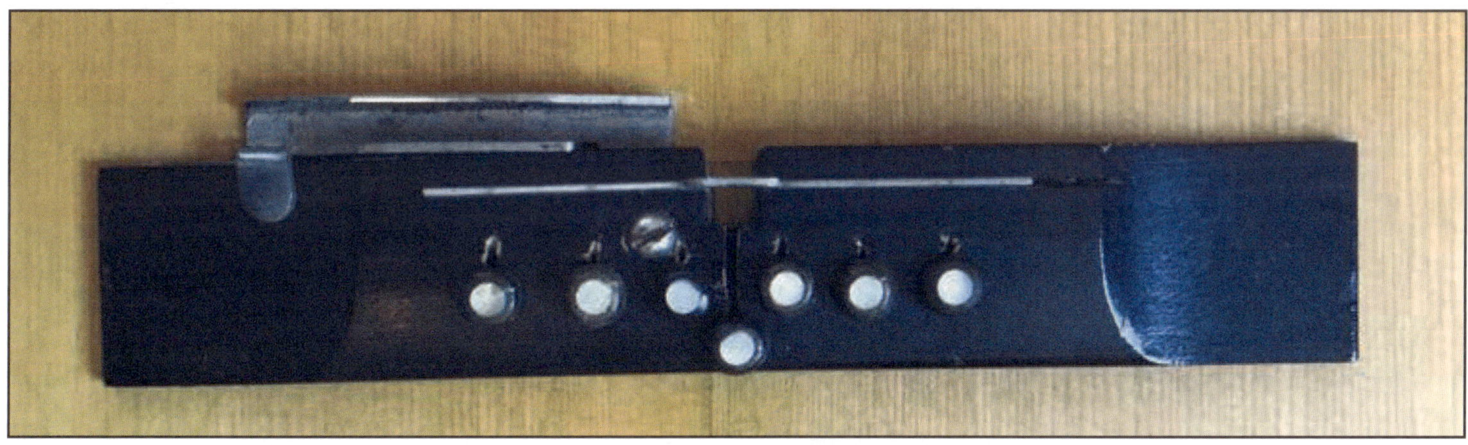

There also has appeared a version of a Custom Built No. 3 as a seven-string guitar set up for lap "Hawaiian"-style playing. Collection/photographs by the author.

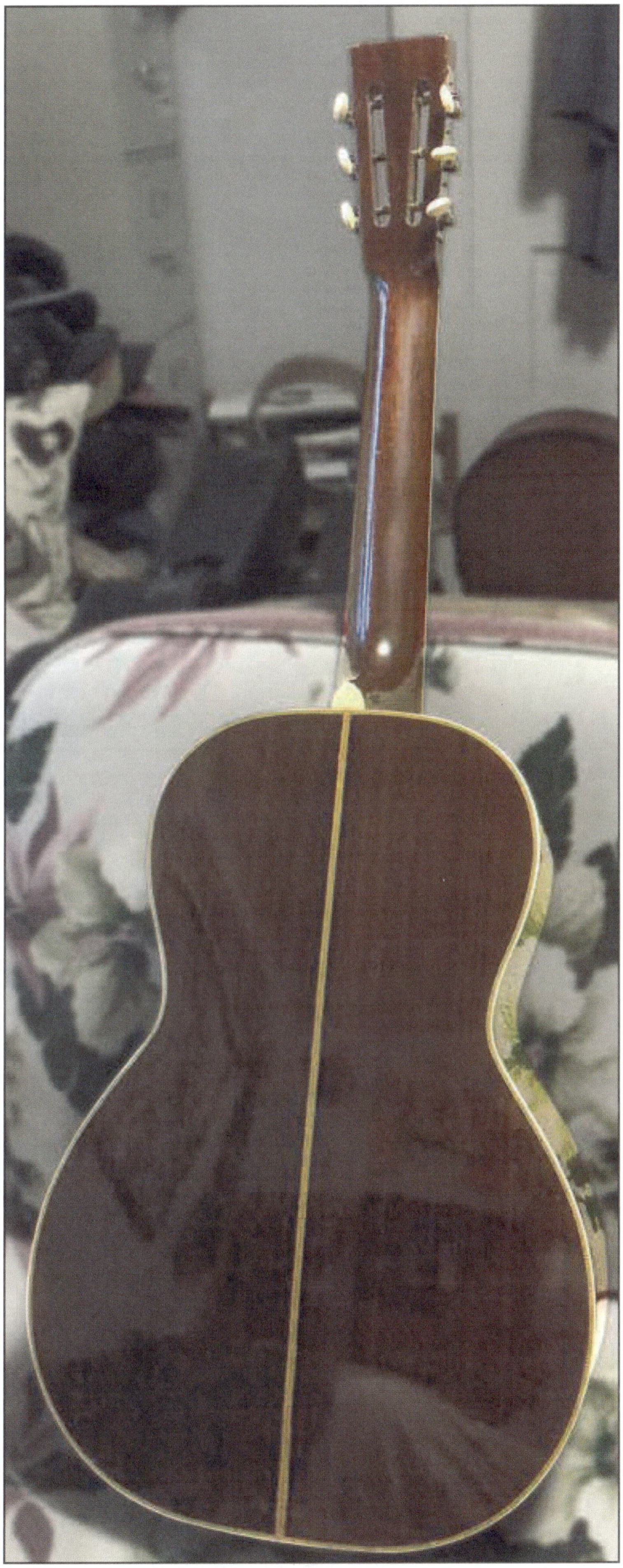

Three fancy Custom Built No. 4's have recently surfaced in the same area of Wisconsin. An additional and similar guitar features a partial vine fingerboard inlay and a bound headstock with "Regal" in pearl script. Collection/photographs by the author.

Faux Wood Grained

Instrument: Flattop guitar.

Model: "The Acorn."

Years Made: 1939-1948?

Brand(s): American Institute, Mid-West Company, Bronson, McKinney, More Harmony, Associated Teachers, The Acorn.

Quality: Low grade.

Special Features: Painted faux wood graining on body.

Woods: Maple neck.

Measurements: 37" long, 24 ¼-½" scale, 4" deep at endpin, 13" lower bout, 9-9 ¼" upper bout, 1 13/16" fingerboard width at nut.

Logos Used: "American Institute" white headstock stencil, "Mid-West Company" white headstock stencil, "McKinney" white headstock stencil, "More Harmony" white headstock stencil, "Associated Teachers" white headstock stencil, "The Acorn" white headstock stencil, Bronson headstock decal, multi colored Regal headstock decal.

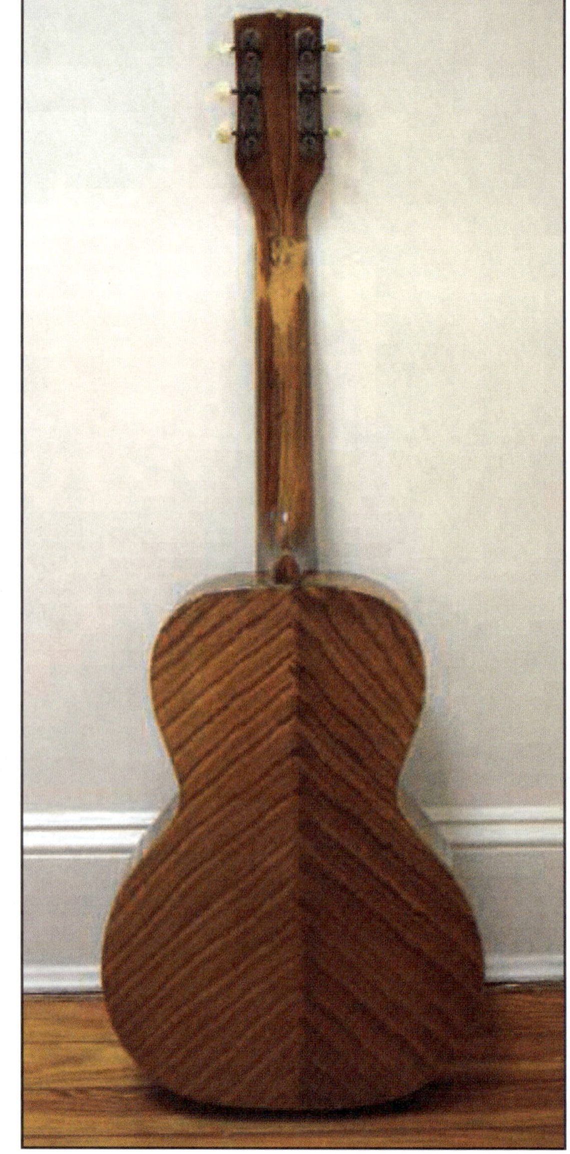

Photographs of front and back of the guitar are courtesy of an eBay seller.

The Washburn Body Used On Other Regal Models.

Instrument: Flattop guitar.

Model: Washburn Solo 5257 style body.

Brand(s): Bostonian, Kingston/Wurlitzer, Broman/Polk, Publix, Marveltone.

Woods: Mahogany top.

Measurements: 24 ¼-25 ½" scale, 14 ⅛-15 3⁄16" lower bout, 9 ½"-10" upper bout.

Logos Used: "Washburn" white stencil on headstock, "Bostonian" white headstock stencil, "Wurlitzer" stamped inside soundhole, "Kingston" silk-screened on headstock in white, "Publix" silkscreened on headstock in white, "Marveltone" in gold script on headstock.

◄Here is just one example of a Washburn body, marked with the model number 5257, joined to a Regal-brand neck. Spruce top, rosewood back and sides ala Washburn join a neck of probably poplar, maple or basswood. Although the body (serial number 700) dates from circa 1935/1936, the tuners are typical of the first half of the 1940s, as is the plastic headstock overlay. Photography by Dave Matchette/Elderly Instruments, courtesy Stan Werbin.

(pages 44-46) Here are pictures of two different Regal-made Orpheum Elite-model guitars, one with a tailpiece and one with a pin bridge. The one with the tailpiece is courtesy of the late Scott Freilich/Top Shelf Music. The second—with a body like the Radio Tone on p212 but with a neck related to the Recording King Jumbo—shows details of the headstock and tuners, along with full front and back shots. It belonged to the author and was photographed by Matthew Spencer.

ORPHEUM
ELITE

Photograph of Jerry Smith, "The Yodeling Cowboy," radio station WHO, Des Moines, Iowa, with his signature model guitar, collection of the author.

Chapter Seven: Archtop Guitars

Roundhole: Carved Top

Instrument: Archtop guitar.

Model: Washburn 5250.

Years Made: 1930-1937?

Brand(s): Washburn.

Quality: High grade.

Measurements: 25 ¼" scale, 1 13/16" wide nut, 4" deep body, 15 ¼" lower bout.

Logos Used: Green headstock decal, paper soundhole label.

Brochure used by Regal to introduce their new roundhole "Guitar with Carved Top." Collection of the author. ►

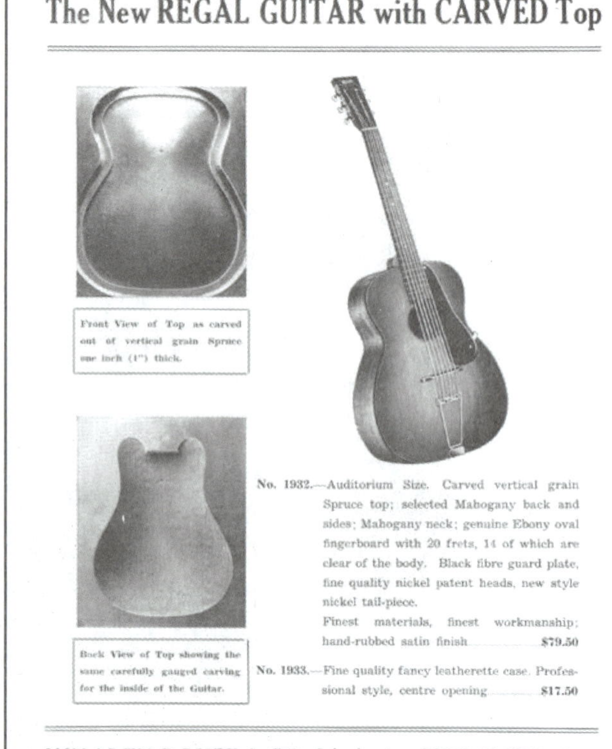

The New REGAL GUITAR with CARVED Top

Front View of Top as carved out of vertical grain Spruce one inch (1") thick.

Back View of Top showing the same carefully gauged carving for the inside of the Guitar.

No. 1932.—Auditorium Size. Carved vertical grain Spruce top; selected Mahogany back and sides; Mahogany neck; genuine Ebony oval fingerboard with 20 frets, 14 of which are clear of the body. Black fibre guard plate, fine quality nickel patent heads, new style nickel tail-piece.
Finest materials, finest workmanship; hand-rubbed satin finish $79.50

No. 1933.—Fine quality fancy leatherette case. Professional style, centre opening $17.50

WHALEY ROYCE & CO., Limited - TORONTO, Ont.

(OVER)

"Le Domino Big Boy." Photographs courtesy Steve Uhrik and Peter Kohman/ Retrofret, Brooklyn, NY.

Roundhole Pressed Top: Le Domino

Model: "Le Domino."

Brand(s): Gretsch (without decalcomania), Supertone (without decalcomania), Bruno.

Quality: Low with high "cool" factor.

Special Features: Decalcomania dominos.

Woods: Birch top.

Logos Used: "Gretsch Jr." in black on white "MOTS" headstock overlay, Supertone headstock decal, Bruno paper soundhole label.

(pages 49-50) Similar to the F Hole: Crown and F Hole: Sultana featured in Regal Musical Instruments Volume One, "Rudy" appears to either have been a custom-order and/or received modifications once it left the Regal facility. Photographs by Matthew Spencer, collection of the author.

RUDY

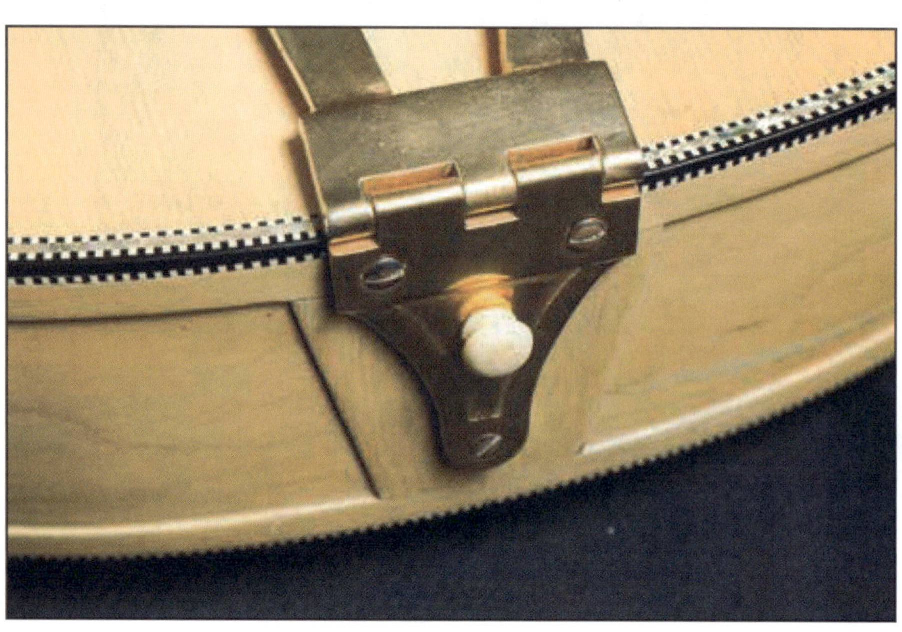

F Hole: Prototype

Instrument: Archtop guitar.

Model: "F" hole.

Years Made: circa 1940.

Quality: High grade.

Special Features: Carved gold tuners, marquetry neck, multiple bindings and inlays.

Woods: Spruce top, maple back and sides.

Measurements: 15 ⅝" at lower bout, 11 ⅛" upper bout, 3 ⅞" deep at end pin, 1 ¾" fingerboard width at nut, 25 7⁄16" scale.

Logos Used: Regal oval metal back of headstock badge.

(pages 51-55) This supposed prototype allegedly came from the estate of the president for Tonk Bros. Regal provided Tonk with the guitar around 1940 as a sample of their high-end work. The body looks suspiciously like that of another Chicago maker, which may have collaborated with Regal on the instrument. The photos show details such as inlay, the marquetry neck, as well as the high-end tuners. Collection/photographs by the author.

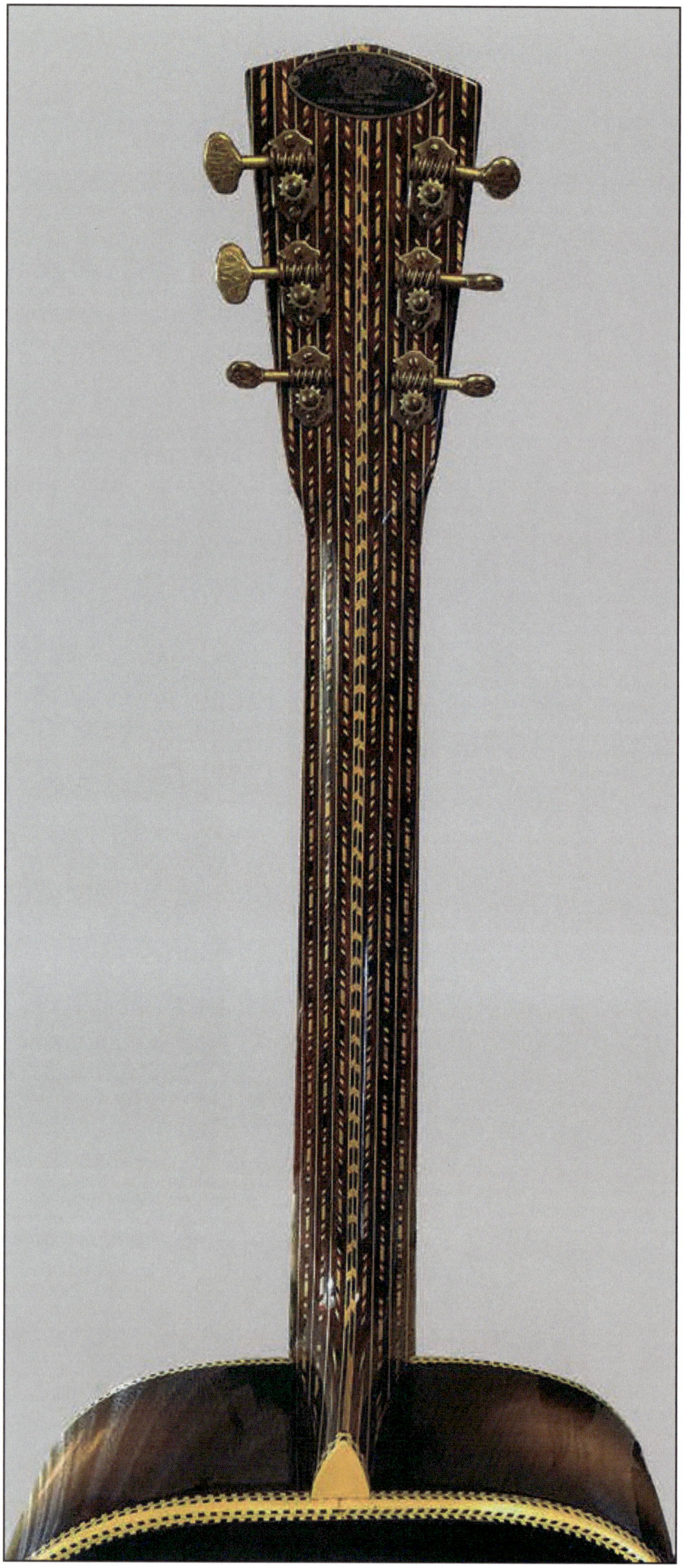

THE MARK OF BETTER INSTRUMENTS
TRADE MARK
Regal
MADE BY
REGAL MUSICAL INSTRUMENT CO.
CHICAGO

Chapter Eight: Ukuleles

TBCO Sterling

Instrument: Ukulele.

Model: Mahogany uke.

Years Made: 1928.

Brand(s): S. S. Stewart, Regal, Sterling.

Quality: Good.

Special Features: Curved fingerboard extension, marquetry.

Woods: Mahogany.

Measurements: Length 20 ½", width 6 3/16", depth 2 ⅜", scale 13 ¼", nut width 1 ¼".

Logos Used: S. S. Stewart soundhole label, paper soundhole label, Sterling headstock decal, T. B. Co. soundhole stamp.

Known Original Wholesale List Price: $12.00.

A marquetry uke, this one branded on the headstock decal▸ and stamped within the soundhole "TB [Tonk Bros.] Co." "Sterling" was a Tonk Bros. house brand. Courtesy Randy Klimpert. Photograph by Amanda Kowalski.

White Bound Mahogany▸

Instrument: Ukulele.

Model: Superior.

Years Made: 1928.

Brand(s): S. S. Stewart, Glee Club/Bruno, Regal.

Quality: High.

Woods: Mahogany.

Measurements: Soprano and Concert.

Logos Used: "S. S. Stewart" in pearl on headstock, "Glee Club" inlayed on headstock in pearl, paper soundhole label, Regal pearl headstock medallion.

Known Original Wholesale List Price: $24.00.

(pages 57-59) There has also turned up a similar soprano-sized instrument of natural finished spruce over rosewood with a mahogany neck. There is added marquetry to the top and soundhole, and a pearl Regal headstock logo. See photographs courtesy Philip Reed for more information.

Regal

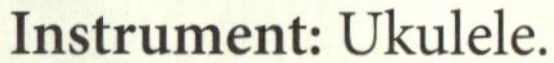

Tonk American

Instrument: Ukulele.

Model: Tonk American.

Years Made: 1927-1930.

Brand(s): Tonk, Wurlitzer.

Quality: Medium grade.

Special Features: Extended fingerboard over top of soundhole.

Woods: Some all mahogany, natural spruce top, dark stained birch back and sides.

Measurements: Concert Size: 12 ⅞" body length, 6 ⅝" lower bout, 5 ⅛" upper bout, 2 ¼" deep.

Logos Used: "Tonk American" headstock decal.

Known Original Wholesale List Price: $9.00-$10.50.

◄*Tonk Bros, ukulele made by Regal, this one labeled "Tonk-American." Courtesy Randy Klimpert. Photograph by Amanda Kowalski.*

A "Whoopee" and "Scroll Stencil" ukulele. Photographs/courtesy Thomas Walsh.

Mapeliene/Scroll Stencil/Whoopee

Instrument: Tenor ukulele.

Model: "Mapeliene," "Scroll Stencil" and "Whoopee."

Years Made: 1930-1934.

Brands: Regal, Sterling, Norwood.

Quality: Low grade.

Special Features: "Scroll" silkscreened on top in various colors; some models lack the scroll silkscreen.

Woods: Birch, maple or mahogany, poplar/basswood neck, some have spruce tops.

Measurements: 14 9⁄16" scale, 2 11⁄16" deep at endpin, 7 ⅝" lower bout at saddle, 5 ⅞" upper bout.

Logos Used: Paper soundhole label.

Le Domino Banjo Ukulele

Instrument: Banjo Ukulele.

Model: "Le Domino."

Brand(s): Le Domino.

Quality: Just okay.

Special Features: Black finish, no tone ring, circle of dominos decalcomania back of resonator, domino decals 3, 5, 7, 10, 12 frets over dots, domino decals between the twelve brackets, original head w/Le Domino logo decal above bridge, and dominos below bridge, bound neck and resonator bottom, dyed wood fb.

Woods: Maple.

Measurements: 8" head, =13 ⅞" scale, 9 ½" resonator.

Logos Used: Medallion headstock decal.

Photographs by Matthew Spencer.

Photographs by Matthew Spencer.

Dancing Couples

Instrument: Ukulele.

Model: Dancing Couples.

Years Made: 1939.

Brand(s): Regal.

Quality: Low grade.

Special Features: Brown to brownish black finish with stenciled mirrored dancing couples, painted top binding.

Woods: Probably birch.

Measurements: "Standard" and "Concert" size.

Logos Used: Green soundhole Regal decal.

Known Original Wholesale List Price: $2.50-$4.00.

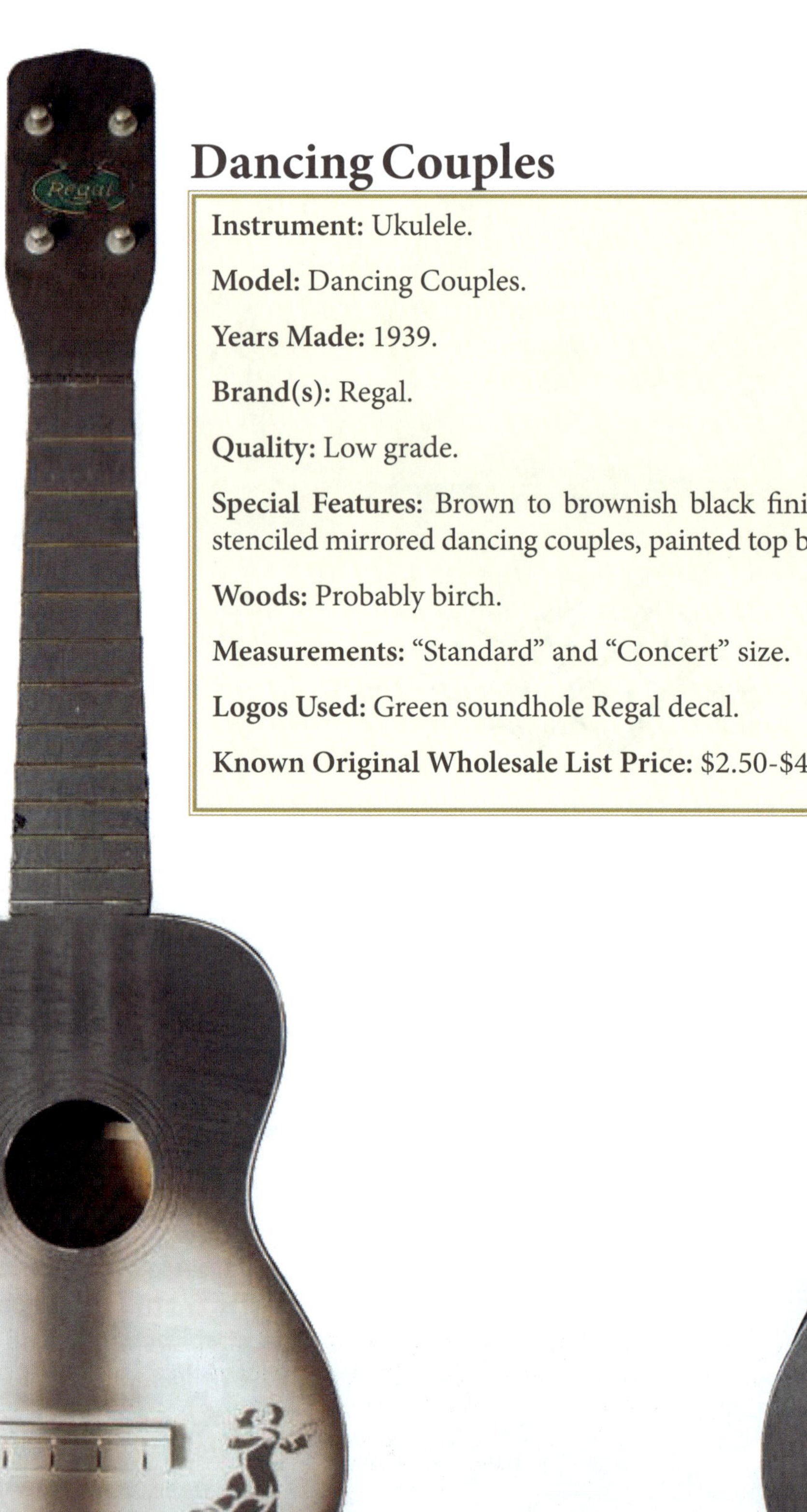

Photographs by Matthew Spencer.

ART DECO model courtesy of Christy and Walter Carter/Carter Vintage Guitars, Nashville, TN, photograph by the author.

June Days

Instrument: Ukulele.

Model: June Days.

Brand(s): Regal.

Quality: Moderate.

Special Features: Decalcomania on face of happy times at the lake.

Woods: All birch, basswood/poplar neck; one example with natural spruce top.

Measurements: Length 20 ¾", width of lower bout 6 ⅝-7 ½", depth 2 ½", scale 13 ¼", nut width 1 ¼".

Logos Used: "June Days" decal on headstock, paper soundhole label.

I've seen two different finishes on the instruments used by Regal for the "June Days" decalcomania ukulele. Photographs courtesy Jake Wildwood/Antebellum Instruments.

June Days

Larger Fretted – A Standard American Musical Instrument.

IT'S TERRIFIC!!

The New

WENDELL HALL
TV UKULELE by Regal

IMMEDIATE DELIVERY

(Yuke – not Ook)

No. 1090 Concert Size Ukulele. Made to the specifications recommended by that great Radio and T-V star, Wendell Hall. New size—new tone—new value. Carefully selected materials throughout. Clear white top. Back and sides in bright two-tone mahogany color. Patent metal pegs. Real NYLON strings.

SPECIAL BONUS—Wendell Hall's regular $1.00 book of instructions and songs free with each Ukulele PLUS a fine felt strumming pick.

Packed six to the carton, with a nice display stand .... **$10.95** EACH LIST

Fine, side-opening, metal-trimmed carrying case .... **$ 4.50** EACH LIST

LESS USUAL TRADE DISCOUNT

SOLD DIRECT FROM FACTORY TO DEALER

SEND YOUR ORDER TO US TODAY SURE!

Be the First to Show This "WENDELL HALL" T-V UKE IN YOUR STORE

REGAL MUSICAL INSTRUMENT CO.

OFFICES and FACTORY: 3211-3215 WEST GRAND AVE., CHICAGO, ILL.

Makers of REGAL . . . Guitars — Mandolins — Ukuleles — String Basses and Electrified Instruments

MUSICAL MERCHANDISE, APRIL, 1950 17

Illustration of Wendell Hall TV Ukulele AD, Musical Merchandise, *April 1950. Collection of the author.*

Palikiko Blues

(Frankie and Johnny)

DIAGRAM ARRANGEMENT FOR HAWAIIAN STEEL GUITAR

As Played By

Arranged by
Harry G. Stanley

Hawaiian Guitar
Duet

THE HONOLULU STRING ENSEMBLE

RADIO AND STAGE ARTISTS
of
IOWA, ILLINOIS and WISCONSIN

Oahu Publishing Company

2108 Payne Ave. - *SOLE DISTRIBUTORS* - Cleveland, Ohio

Price 50¢

No. 199

Made in U. S. A.

Sheet music, "Palikiko Blues," As Played By The Honolulu String Ensemble. From the Oahu Publishing Company. Basso guitarist stands in the back row, second from left. Collection of the author.

Grossman No. 3475

Instrument: Tiple

Model: Grossman No 3475

Years Made: 1928-1949.

Brand: Regal.

Quality: Low Grade.

Special Features: Upgraded version of Schultz No. 2350 added wood marquetry top and soundhole binding, along with a vinyl headstock overlay and fingerboard.

Woods: Natural spruce top, birch back and sides, basswood/poplar neck.

Measurements: 8 ¾-9" at lower bout, 6 ½-¾" at upper bout, 3-3 ³⁄₃₂" deep, scale measures 17", nut measures 1 and ½".

Logos Used: Green headstock decal (1937-1949), paper soundhole label.

Known Original Wholesale List Price: $11.00-14.50.

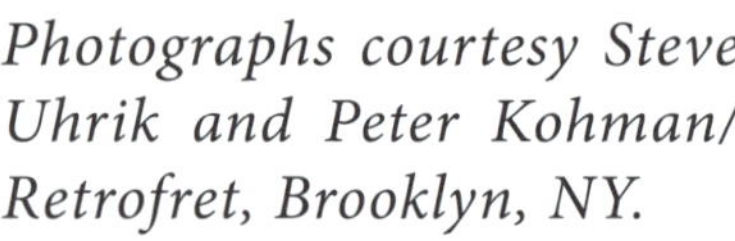

Photographs courtesy Steve Uhrik and Peter Kohman/ Retrofret, Brooklyn, NY.

Photograph by Matthew Spencer

TRADE MARK
Regal
MUSICAL INSTRUMENTS
1895 - 1955
by Bob Carlin
Regal
CENTERSTREAM®